AMAZING ANIMALS
MEERKATS

BY KATE RIGGS

CREATIVE EDUCATION • CREATIVE PAPERBACKS

Published by Creative Education
and Creative Paperbacks
P.O. Box 227, Mankato, Minnesota 56002
Creative Education and Creative Paperbacks
are imprints of The Creative Company
www.thecreativecompany.us

Design by The Design Lab
Production by Rachel Klimpel
Art direction by Rita Marshall
Printed in the United States of America

Photographs by Alamy (JEAN-FR@NCOIS DUCASSE,
petrographer), Corbis (Vincent Grafhorst/Minden Pictures),
Dreamstime (Andre Klaassen, Zuberka), Getty (Steve Clancy
Photography, Martin Harvey, Ioannis Tsotras), iStock (Farinosa,
slowmotiongli, Snowshill), Shutterstock (Aaron Amat, anetapics,
EcoPrint, Eric Isselee, Michael Maes)

Library of Congress Cataloging-in-Publication Data
Names: Riggs, Kate, author.
Title: Meerkats / by Kate Riggs.
Description: Mankato, Minnesota : Creative Education and Cre-
ative Paperbacks, [2023] | Series: Amazing animals | Includes
bibliographical references and index. | Audience: Ages 6–9 |
Audience: Grades 2–3 | Summary: "Elementary-aged readers
will discover how meerkats stay safe from predators. Full color
images and clear explanations highlight the habitat, diet, and
lifestyle of these fascinating African mammals."-- Provided by
publisher.
Identifiers: LCCN 2021057281 (print) | LCCN 2021057282
(ebook) | ISBN 9781640265707 (hardcover) | ISBN
9781682771259 (paperback) | ISBN 9781640006898
(ebook)
Subjects: LCSH: Meerkat--Juvenile literature.
Classification: LCC QL737.C235 R54 2023 (print) |
LCC QL737.C235 (ebook) | DDC 599.74/2--dc23/
eng/20211220
LC record available at https://lccn.loc.gov/2021057281
LC ebook record available at https://lccn.loc.
gov/2021057282

Table of Contents

Meerkats belong to the same animal family as mongooses.

Meerkats are small mammals. They stand on their back legs to watch for danger. If an eagle or hawk flies over, the meerkats dive into their burrows to hide.

burrows holes or tunnels dug in the ground for use as a home

mammals animals that have hair or fur and feed their babies with milk

Dark eye circles reflect,
or throw back, the
bright sunlight.

Meerkats have long, thin bodies. They usually have brown fur with black patches around their eyes. Long, sharp claws on their toes help them dig burrows and catch **prey.**

prey animals that are killed and eaten by other animals

Most meerkats grow to around 12 inches (30.5 cm). Their tails are almost as long as their bodies. They weigh about as much as a basketball.

Stripes on a meerkat's back are different on each animal.

Meerkats live in hot, dry areas of southern Africa. It can get up to 113 °F (45 °C) there during the day. At night, the temperature can drop to 40 °F (4.4 °C). Meerkats' burrows stay cool in the daytime. Their burrows are warm at night.

Meerkats have ears that can pinch shut to keep out sand.

A good sense of smell helps a meerkat find food anywhere.

Meerkats dig up **insects** to eat. Their favorites are grasshoppers, beetles, and **larvae**. Meerkats eat lizards and **rodents**, too. They even munch on dangerous scorpions!

insects small animals with three body parts and six legs

larvae the form some animals take when they hatch from eggs, before changing into their adult form

rodents small mammals with big teeth, such as mice and rats

Young meerkats do not go far from the burrow.

A meerkat mother gives birth to four to six **pups**. The pups cannot see or hear when they are born. They stay in the burrow and drink their mother's milk. After almost four weeks, the pups go outside. Meerkats live about 10 years in the wild.

pups baby meerkats

A male and female called the alpha pair lead the mob.

Meerkats live in family groups called mobs. Up to 40 meerkats live in a mob. Each mob guards its own **territory**. If two mobs meet, the meerkats will fight.

territory a space that is the home of one animal or one group of animals

Meerkats spend most of the day looking for food. One meerkat serves as the lookout. The lookout watches for danger. It barks or chirps to the others. Meerkats spend time cleaning each other's fur and playing, too.

Meerkats look for insects in trees and other nest sites.

Some people travel to Africa to see meerkats in the wild. Others see them on TV or at zoos. It can be fun to watch these furry little mammals scurry around!

Meerkats love being in a group instead of by themselves.

A Meerkat Tale

People in Africa told a story about why meerkats are always on the lookout. They said that Meerkat never watched where she was going. The other animals told her to be more careful. They warned her not to wake the Sleeping Stones. But one day, she crashed into the Stones. The Stones told her that, from then on, she would have to be the lookout for all animals.

Read More

Emminizer, Theresa. *Burrowing Meerkats*. New York: PowerKids Press, 2021.

Golkar, Golriz. *Meerkats*. Minneapolis: Pop!, a divsion of ABDO, 2021.

Nichols, Rhonda E. *Meerkats*. Minneapolis: Kaleidoscope, 2021.

Websites

National Geographic Kids: Meerkat Facts!
https://www.natgeokids.com/au/discover/animals/general-animals/meerkat-facts/
Discover meerkat facts here.

San Diego Zoo Kids: Meerkat
https://sdzwildlifeexplorers.org/animals/meerkat
Learn more about meerkat pups and adults.

Note: Every effort has been made to ensure that the websites listed above are suitable for children, that they have educational value, and that they contain no inappropriate material. However, because of the nature of the Internet, it is impossible to guarantee that these sites will remain active indefinitely or that their contents will not be altered.

Index